HOW TO TRAIN YOUR PET BRAIN

by **NELLY BUCHET**

illustrated by **AMY JINDRA**

beaming books

MINNEAPOLIS

For my good boy Sacha
—N.B.

28 27 26 25 24 23 22   1 2 3 4 5 6 7 8

Art direction by Nicholas Schlavensky

ISBN: 978-1-5064-8050-3
eISBN: 978-1-5064-8170-8

Library of Congress Cataloging-in-Publication Data

Names: Buchet, Nelly, author. | Jindra, Amy, illustrator.
Title: How to train your pet brain / by Nelly Buchet ; illustrated by Amy
   Jindra.
Description: Minneapolis, Minnesota : Beaming Books, an imprint of 1517
   Media, [2022]. | Audience: Ages 5-8. | Summary: "With heart and humor,
   How to Train Your Pet Brain welcomes kids to explore how their bodies
   and minds work together to process emotions. Lighthearted illustrations
   paired with grounded language help kids understand why their brain does
   what it does, that big feelings are OK, and a strategy to help feel
   calm"-- Provided by publisher.
Identifiers: LCCN 2021018981 (print) | LCCN 2021018982 (ebook) | ISBN
   9781506480503 (hardcover) | ISBN 9781506481708 (ebook)
Subjects: LCSH: Brain--Juvenile literature. | Mind and body--Juvenile
   literature. | Emotion recognition--Juvenile literature.
Classification: LCC QP376 .B83 2022 (print) | LCC QP376 (ebook) | DDC
   612.8/2--dc23
LC record available at https://lccn.loc.gov/2021018981
LC ebook record available at https://lccn.loc.gov/2021018982

VN0004589; 9781506480503; JAN2022

Beaming Books
PO Box 1209
Minneapolis, MN 55440-1209
Beamingbooks.com

Your brain is like a pet.

It even has a tail—your spinal cord—
that runs down your back and connects
your thoughts to your body.

That's how your body knows what to do.
Your body listens to what you're thinking.
And your pet brain listens to your body.
It goes both ways.

BRAIN TRAINING 101

YOUR BRAIN AND YOU

YOUR BRAIN

When you frown and stick out your bottom lip, you don't feel great.

But when you smile . . .

big,

bigger,

HUGE,

to show ALL your
shiny teeth,

how do you feel?

Pretty happy, wonderful,
and bright, right?

Well, congratulations!
You just taught your brain a new trick!
You changed how you feel.

And you can do that
anytime, anywhere.

But it's not always easy to train your pet brain.

It takes practice . . .

and patience.

Like any pet, your brain has habits you might not like:

it can be stubborn,

keep you up at night,

or feel out of control.

But you can train your pet brain,
and understand when it tries to protect you.

Having an upset brain is no fun.
You might get super angry or super sad—
sometimes for what feels like no reason
at all.

There's nothing wrong with those feelings.
It's GOOD to feel a lot.
It means you care!

But big feelings can make it hard to talk to
your pet brain.

You have to let the feelings out first, with a wiggle,

a howl,

or a giggle.

And before you know it, they will pass.

So if you want to train your brain,
you need to choose a good time to learn:
when you are calm.

YOGA IN
THE PARK
4–5PM

And you can feel calm when you breathe slowly and deeply.
You can do it wherever and whenever.
Like now.

Close your eyes and breathe in
deeply through your nose,

then breathe out as slowly as you can.

Doesn't that feel nice?

Now your pet brain is
ready to learn a new trick,

or fact,

or game.

Because your pet brain
needs to play too.

When your pet brain feels
good, so do you.

So take care of your pet brain,

and it'll take care of you!

ABOUT THE AUTHOR AND ILLUSTRATOR

NELLY BUCHET is the author of ALA Notable Book *Cat Dog Dog: The Story of a Blended Family* and the four-boardbook Can't Do series. She holds a degree from McGill University, where she created a nonprofit project that brings picture books to refugee children through orphanages and libraries. She splits her time between Los Angeles and Berlin.

AMY JINDRA is a designer and illustrator who enjoys developing characters and scenes that tell a story, create a connection, and warm the heart. She lives in Cleveland, Ohio.